Inglés sin Barreras®

El Video-Maestro de Inglés Conversacional

4 El calendario y el clima

Cuaderno de ejercicios

ISBN: 1-59172-306-X I704WB04

El calendario y el clima

Índice

No se olvide de estudiar las lecciones en el manual antes de hacer los ejercicios de este cuaderno.

Examen inicial

Antes de comenzar el estudio de este volumen, dedique unos minutos a contestar a las 15 preguntas del examen siguiente. Llene el círculo correspondiente a la respuesta correcta.

1. *February 14, 2003 ________*
O a) 14/3/2002
O b) 2/14/2004
O c) 2003/14/2
O d) 2003/2/14
O e) 2/14/2003

2. *His birthday is 12/16. _______*
O a) November eleventh
O b) December 16th
O c) December 11th
O d) December twelfth
O e) November 15th

3. *April, ________________*
O a) May, June, July
O b) September, October, December
O c) January, March, August
O d) May, July, August
O e) March, May, June

4. *Today is August 15th. ________ August 13th.*
O a) Yesterday was
O b) Tomorrow is
O c) The day before yesterday was
O d) The day before yesterday
O e) The day after tomorrow is

5. *They__________ all weekend.*
O a) was shopping
O b) wasn't
O c) shopping
O d) were shopping
O e) isn't shopping

6. *____ you ____ yesterday at 3:00?*
O a) Did, calling
O b) Do, sleeping
O c) Were, sleeping
O d) Are, sleep
O e) Is, sleep

7. Was he sick yesterday? _______
O a) No, he was.
O b) No, he wasn't.
O c) Sick.
O d) Yes, sick.
O e) Yes, yesterday.

8. *There was __ outside this morning.*
O a) snow
O b) rainy
O c) clouds
O d) sunny
O e) storms

9. *________________ cloudy?*
O a) Are there
O b) Is there
O c) Are they
O d) Is it
O e) Was there

10. *Was it sunny on Saturday?*
O a) No, there weren't.
O b) Yes, it was.
O c) Yes, it is.
O d) Yes, it does.
O e) No, it isn't.

11. *The temperature is ________.*
O a) 36th
O b) the 36º
O c) thirty-sixth degree
O d) about 36
O e) 36º

12. *_____ it was windy and cold.*
O a) Last weekend
O b) Next weekend
O c) Next Thursday
O d) A little
O e) Tomorrow

13. *I _____ my book all morning.*
O a) stopped
O b) listened to
O c) looked for
O d) arrived
O e) traveled

14. *___ he ___English last year?*
O a) Did, studying
O b) Do, studying
O c) Did, study
O d) Do, learn
O e) Does, studying

15. *Did you go to school yesterday?*
____
O a) No, to school.
O b) No, I did.
O c) No, today.
O d) Yes, I did.
O e) To school.

Cuando haya estudiado todas las lecciones de este volumen, haga el mismo examen de nuevo. Lo encontrará al final de este cuaderno, en la página titulada "Examen final".

Compare los resultados obtenidos en este examen con los del examen final. Así comprobará lo que ha aprendido y podrá medir su progreso.

Cuando haya terminado este examen, empiece a estudiar la Lección uno.

Lección 1

Months of the Year
January
February
March
April
May
June
July
August
September
October
November
December

1 Notas

Vocabulario 1

Encontrará las respuestas en la página 11.

A. Escriba la palabra completa después de cada palabra abreviada. Haga un círculo alrededor de las palabras que no estén abreviadas.

Ejemplo: Jan. *January*

1. Tue. ________________
2. Oct. ________________
3. May ________________
4. Wed. ________________
5. Thu. ________________
6. Dec. ________________
7. July ________________
8. Apr. ________________
9. Feb. ________________
10. Sat. ________________
11. Sept. ________________
12. Nov. ________________

Encontrará las respuestas en la página 11.

B. Sopa de letras
En el cuadro de abajo se incluyen las palabras correspondientes a los meses del año. Encuentre estas palabras teniendo en cuenta que se leen de arriba abajo y de izquierda a derecha.

January, February, March, April, May, June, July, August, September, ~~October~~, November, December

O	C	T	O	B	E	R	F	Y	R	N
S	E	P	T	E	M	B	E	R	M	O
D	J	A	O	X	H	R	B	V	N	V
E	M	P	T	U	M	A	R	C	H	E
C	F	R	P	M	J	J	U	N	E	M
E	C	I	U	T	T	U	A	S	L	B
M	J	L	L	J	R	T	R	B	E	E
B	J	A	N	U	A	R	Y	B	E	R
E	U	A	C	L	A	U	G	U	S	T
R	N	M	A	Y	D	F	G	W	R	S

Encontrará las respuestas en la página 12.

C. Haga una línea que una la fecha de la columna de la izquierda con la fecha correspondiente de la columna de la derecha.

Ejemplo:	June 6, 2001 ________________	6/6/2001
1.	February 3, 1950	7/4/76
2.	Aug. 8, 2002	11/7/14
3.	July 11, 2014	3/2/1950
4.	March 17, 1994	1/1/00
5.	October 29, 2009	8/8/02
6.	April 17, 1994	2/3/50
7.	Jan. 1, 2000	10/29/2009
8.	Nov. 7, 2014	4/17/1994
9.	July 4, 1976	7/11/14
10.	March 2, 1950	3/17/94

Encontrará las respuestas en la página 12.

D. Escriba oraciones usando las fechas indicadas a continuación.

Ejemplo: Martha 4/4

Her birthday is April fourth.

1. José 9/1

____

2. Sheila 4/12

____

3. Tina 5/3 Tony 5/3

____

4. Jim 11/11

____

5. Patricia 1/7

____

6. Kim 7/2 Kelly 7/2

____

7. Ángela 8/8

____

8. Joe 2/4

____

Diálogo 1

Encontrará las respuestas en la página 13.

Llene los espacios en blanco.

Randy	___________ is my birthday.
Lavinia	It is? Today is my husband's birthday, ___________.
Randy	Oh. ___________ husband's birthday is on April 11th?
Lavinia	Yes. Guess when my birthday is?
Randy	I don't know. ___________?
Lavinia	My birthday is April 12th.
Randy	You're kidding.
Lavinia	Nope. My ___________ is tomorrow.
Randy	Do ___________ and your husband celebrate together?
Lavinia	Yes, we usually have one party.
Randy	That sounds like fun.
Lavinia	It is. Can you join us? We're having the party tonight.
Randy	Thank ___________, but my wife is taking ___________ out to dinner.
Lavinia	Oh, well. Next year!
Randy	Yes, next ___________.

1 Examen

Encontrará las respuestas en la página 13.

Llene los espacios en blanco con el tipo de fecha correcta.

Ejemplo:	March 10, 1966	3/10/66	March 10th
1.	January 3, 2010	______________	______________
2.	______________________	10/11/2017	______________
3.	April 1, 1999	______________	______________
4.	______________, 2002	______________	June 4th
5.	______________________	2/7/93	______________
6.	August 10, 2001	______________	______________

Vocabulario

A.

1. Tuesday
2. October
3. May
4. Wednesday
5. Thursday
6. December
7. July
8. April
9. February
10. Saturday
11. September
12. November

B.

O	C	T	O	B	E	R	F	Y	R	N
S	E	P	T	E	M	B	E	R	M	O
D	J	A	O	X	H	R	B	V	N	V
E	M	P	T	U	M	A	R	C	H	E
C	F	R	P	M	J	J	U	N	E	M
E	C	I	U	T	T	U	A	S	L	B
M	J	L	L	J	R	T	R	B	E	E
B	J	A	N	U	A	R	Y	B	E	R
E	U	A	C	L	A	U	G	U	S	T
R	N	M	A	Y	D	F	G	W	R	S

Clase

C.

1.	February 3, 1950	2/3/50
2.	Aug. 8, 2002	8/8/02
3.	July 11, 2014	7/11/14
4.	March 17, 1994	3/17/94
5.	October 29, 2009	10/29/2009
6.	April 17, 1994	4/17/1994
7.	Jan. 1, 2000	1/1/00
8.	Nov. 7, 2014	11/7/14
9.	July 4, 1976	7/4/76
10.	March 2, 1950	3/2/1950

D.

1. His birthday is September first.
2. Her birthday is April twelfth.
3. Their birthdays are May third.
4. His birthday is November eleventh.
5. Her birthday is January seventh.
6. Their birthdays are July second.
7. Her birthday is August eighth.
8. His birthday is February fourth.

Diálogo

Randy	Today is my birthday.
Lavinia	It is? Today is my husband's birthday, too.
Randy	Oh. Your husband's birthday is on April 11th?
Lavinia	Yes. Guess when my birthday is?
Randy	I don't know. When?
Lavinia	My birthday is April 12th.
Randy	You're kidding.
Lavinia	Nope. My birthday is tomorrow.
Randy	Do you and your husband celebrate together?
Lavinia	Yes, we usually have one party.
Randy	That sounds like fun.
Lavinia	It is. Can you join us? We're having a party tonight.
Randy	Thank you, but my wife is taking me out to dinner.
Lavinia	Oh, well. Next year!
Randy	Yes, next year.

Examen

1.	January 3, 2010	1/3/10	January 3rd
2.	October 11, 2017	10/11/2017	October 11th
3.	April 1, 1999	4/1/99	April 1st
4.	June 4, 2002	6/4/2002	June 4th
5.	February 7, 1993	2/7/93	February 7th
6.	August 10, 2001	8/10/01	August 10th

Lección 2

Inglés sin Barreras
fox
watch
bush
class
foxes
watches
bushes
classes

2 Notas

Vocabulario 2

Encontrará las respuestas en la página 24.

A. Complete las oraciones relacionadas con los calendarios.

Ejemplo: Yesterday was June 26th. Tomorrow is June 28th.

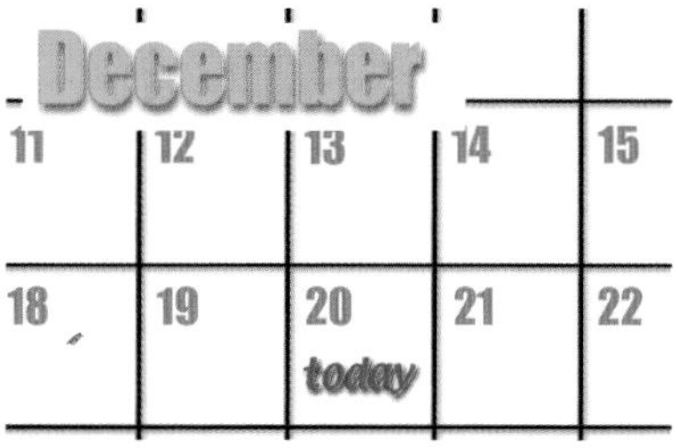

1. ________________ December 18th.
2. Tomorrow ________________

3. The day after tomorrow ________________
4. Yesterday ________________

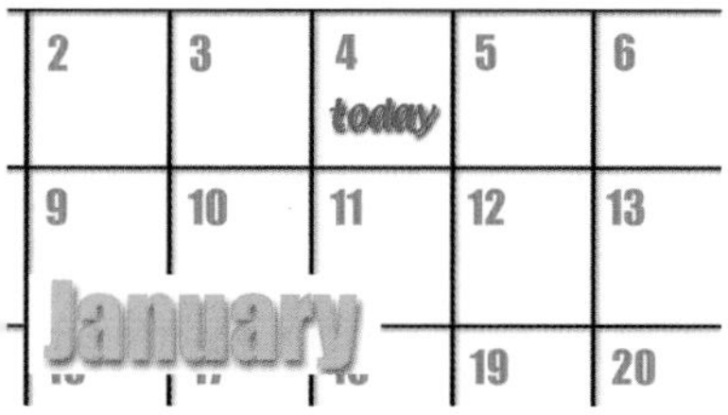

5. ________________ January 2nd.
6. The day after tomorrow ________________

7. ________________ October 29th.
8. Tomorrow ________________

Encontrará las respuestas en la página 24.

B. Llene los espacios en blanco. En la columna de la izquierda, use letras para escribir los números que sirven para ordenar. En la columna de la derecha, use la forma abreviada de dichos números.

Ejemplo:	forty-fourth	44th
	ninety-second	92nd
1.	sixty-third	____________
2.	____________	35th
3.	____________	20th
4.	twenty-first	____________
5.	____________	48th
6.	____________	77th
7.	____________	99th
8.	fifty-second	____________

Clase 2

Encontrará las respuestas en la página 24.

C. Complete las oraciones relacionadas con los dibujos.

Ejemplo: He was running at 4:30 yesterday.

1. ______________________ all weekend.

2. ______________________ at 7:15 AM.

3. ______________________ last night at 8:00 PM.

4. ______________________ at 6:30.

5. ______________________ all day.

6. ______________________ last Sunday afternoon.

Encontrará las respuestas en la página 24.

D. Escriba las preguntas que corresponden a estas respuestas. Use las palabras entre paréntesis.

Ejemplo: (last Saturday) What was he doing last Saturday?
He was playing baseball.

1. (sick yesterday) ______________________________
   Yes, she was.

2. (studying at 11:00 PM) ______________________________
   ____
   No, he wasn't.

3. (what) ______________________________
   They were reading.

4. (living in New York last year) ______________________________
   ____
   No, they weren't.

5. (you, yesterday afternoon) ______________________________
   ____
   I was sleeping.

6. (you, reading a book) ______________________________
   ____
   Yes, we were.

Encontrará las respuestas en la página 25.

Seleccione la respuesta más adecuada.

Andy Good morning, Sasha. How are you?
Sasha I'm fine. And you?
Andy a) Me? I'm great.
b) You? I'm great.

Sasha Where were you yesterday afternoon?
Andy a) At 3:00?
b) At what time?
Sasha About 3:00.

Andy I was at home.
Sasha I was calling and calling. You weren't at home.
Andy a) Yes, I was.
b) No. I was.

Sasha What were you doing?
Andy I was watching TV.
Sasha a) What were you doing?
b) What were you watching?

Andy A soccer game. The TV was very loud.
Sasha No wonder. You didn't hear the phone!
Andy a) You're probably right!
b) You're probably wrong.

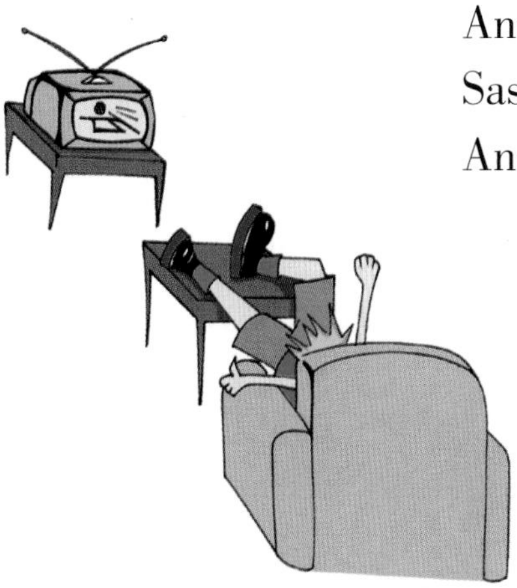

2 Examen

Encontrará las respuestas en la página 25.

Escriba oraciones que describan los dibujos. Use las palabras entre paréntesis.

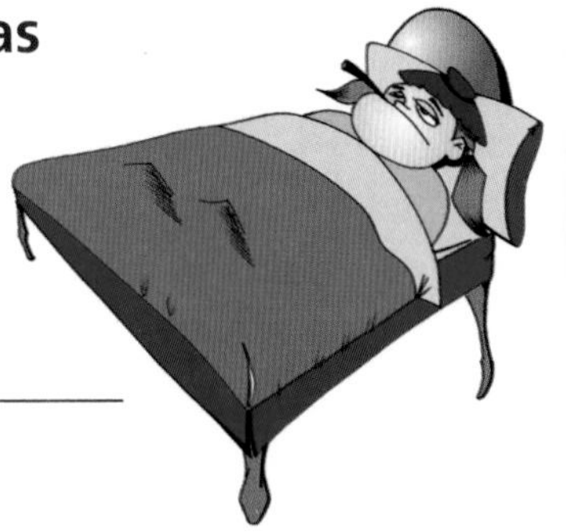

Ejemplo: (last Saturday)

She was sick last Saturday.

1. (the day before yesterday)

____

____

2. (last night at 10:30 PM)

____

____

3. (last Wednesday)

____

____

4. (in the morning)

____

____

Encontrará las respuestas en la página 25.

5. (7:00 AM)

____

____

6. (last month)

____

____

7. (all day yesterday)

____

____

8. (at 4:00 PM)

____

____

Respuestas

Vocabulario

A.
1. The day before yesterday was December 18th.
2. Tomorrow is December 21st.
3. The day after tomorrow is August 25th.
4. Yesterday was August 22nd.
5. The day before yesterday was January 2nd.
6. The day after tomorrow is January 6th.
7. Yesterday was October 29th.
8. Tomorrow is October 31st.

B.
1. 63rd
2. thirty-fifth
3. twentieth
4. 21st
5. forty-eighth
6. seventy-seventh
7. ninety-ninth
8. 52nd

Clase

C.
1. She was shopping all weekend.
2. They were eating at 7:15 AM.
3. She was writing last night at 8:00 PM.
4. She was cooking at 6:30.
5. He was sitting all day.
6. They were playing soccer last Sunday afternoon.

D.
1. Was she sick yesterday?
2. Was he studying at 11:00 PM?
3. What were they doing?
4. Were they living in New York last year?
5. What were you doing yesterday afternoon?
6. Were you reading a book?

Diálogo

Andy	Good morning, Sasha. How are you?
Sasha	I'm fine. And you?
Andy	a) Me? I'm great.
Sasha	Where were you yesterday afternoon?
Andy	b) At what time?
Sasha	About 3:00.
Andy	I was at home.
Sasha	I was calling and calling. You weren't at home.
Andy	a) Yes, I was.
Sasha	What were you doing?
Andy	I was watching TV.
Sasha	b) What were you watching?
Andy	A soccer game. The TV was very loud.
Sasha	No wonder. You didn't hear the phone!
Andy	a) You're probably right!

Examen

1. She was working the day before yesterday.
2. They were talking last night at 10:30 PM.
3. They were angry last Wednesday.
4. They were playing soccer in the morning.
5. He was getting up at 7:00 AM.
6. She was tired last month.
7. He was thinking all day yesterday.
8. She was playing at 4:00 PM.

Lección 3

3 Notas

Vocabulario 3

Encontrará las respuestas en la página 36.

A. Llene los espacios en blanco usando palabras de la lista siguiente.

rain	rainy	clouds	cloudy
snow	snowy	wind	windy
sun	sunny	~~storm~~	~~stormy~~

Ejemplo: Is it stormy?

Yes, there's a big storm here.

1. There are many ______

   It is very ______

2. It was ______ last night.

   There was ______ on the ground this morning.

3. Was it ______ yesterday?

   No, there was no ______

4. Is the ______ out?

   No, it isn't ______

5. There is no ______ in July.

   It's usually ______ in January.

3 Vocabulario

Encontrará las respuestas en la página 36.

B. Ponga las letras en orden.

Ejemplo: nauumt ___autumn___

1. dmhui ___h___
2. eeahwtr ___w___
3. tmyros ___s___
4. gtnnigilh ___l___
5. mmresu ___s___
6. nnusy ___s___
7. dneruth ___t___
8. nertwi ___w___

Encontrará las respuestas en la página 36.

C. Conteste a las preguntas relacionadas con el calendario. Use respuestas cortas.

Ejemplo: Is it raining today?

Yes, it is.

1. Was it sunny on Monday?

____

2. Did it rain on Monday?

____

3. Did it snow on Sunday?

____

Encontrará las respuestas en la página 36.

4. Was it windy last Sunday?

5. Was it raining on Tuesday?

6. Is it foggy today?

7. Was there lightning on Monday?

8. Was it cold on Monday?

Encontrará las respuestas en la página 36.

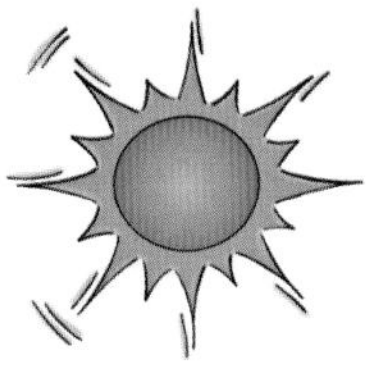

D. Escriba las palabras relacionadas con cada estación en la columna correspondiente. Haga este ejercicio basándose en su experiencia personal; en este caso, hay varias respuestas correctas.

cool	humid	clear	sunny	hot
rainy	snowy	windy	foggy	warm
lightning	storm	cool	dry	cloudy

winter	spring	summer	autumn
______	______	______	______
______	______	______	______
______	______	______	______
______	______	______	______
______	______	______	______
______	______	______	______

3 Diálogo

Encontrará las respuestas en la página 37.

En este diálogo protagonizado por John y Samantha, relacione cada oración con el personaje correspondiente.

Tom		Samantha
✔	How was your vacation?	______
______	It was terrible.	______
______	Why?	______
______	The weather was bad.	______
______	It rained on Friday and Saturday.	______
______	How about the weekend?	______
______	It was cloudy and cold.	______
______	There was a big storm on Saturday night.	______
______	Was there thunder?	______
______	A little.	______
______	I'm sorry to hear that.	______
______	Yes, the weather was bad every day!	______

Examen 3

Encontrará las respuestas en la página 37.

Llene los espacios en blanco. Las oraciones están relacionadas con el calendario.

Ejemplo: On Sunday the temperature was 36°.

1. ______________________ it was very windy.

2. On Monday ______________________

3. ______________________ it was sunny and 57°.

4. ______________________ it was a little sunny and 47°.

5. On Friday it was a little ______________________

6. Today ______________________

3 Respuestas

Vocabulario

A.
1. There are many clouds.
   It is very cloudy.
2. It was rainy last night.
   There was rain on the ground this morning.
3. Was it windy yesterday?
   No, there was no wind.
4. Is the sun shining?
   No, it isn't sunny.
5. There is no snow in July.
   It's usually snowy in January.

B.
1. humid
2. weather
3. stormy
4. lightning
5. summer
6. sunny
7. thunder
8. winter

Clase

C.
1. Yes, it was.
2. No, it didn't.
3. No, it didn't.
4. No, it wasn't.
5. No, it wasn't.
6. No, it isn't.
7. No, there wasn't.
8. No, it wasn't.

D.

En este ejercicio, se aceptan todas las respuestas.

Respuestas 3

Diálogo

Tom	Samantha
How was your vacation?	
	It was terrible.
Why?	
	The weather was bad. It rained on Friday and Saturday.
How about the weekend?	
	It was cloudy and cold. There was a big storm on Saturday night.
Was there thunder?	
	A little.
I'm sorry to hear that.	
	Yes, the weather was bad every day!

Examen

1. On Tuesday it was very windy.
2. On Monday it snowed.
3. On Thursday it was sunny and 57º.
4. On Wednesday it was a little sunny and 47º.
5. On Friday it was a little foggy.
6. Today it is sunny and 60º.

4 Notas

Lección 4

Then, it started to storm. We watched the lightning and listened to the thunder. I was a little scared. I wanted to go home.

4 Notas

Encontrará las respuestas en la página 48.

A. Ponga los verbos en tiempo pasado.

Ejemplo: shop *shopped*

1. try ______________________
2. play ______________________
3. look for ______________________
4. pack ______________________
5. stop ______________________
6. listen ______________________
7. arrive ______________________
8. travel ______________________
9. call ______________________
10. want ______________________
11. show ______________________
12. study ______________________

Encontrará las respuestas en la página 48.

B. Haga oraciones negativas.

Ejemplo: He called me last night.

He didn't call me last night.

1. He played basketball.

___

2. They shopped all day.

___

3. We walked a lot.

___

4. I packed yesterday.

___

5. She talked to her sister on Tuesday.

___

6. They listened to the radio.

___

7. It rained last weekend.

___

8. You looked for it all morning.

___

Encontrará las respuestas en la página 48.

C. Haga preguntas con cada una de las oraciones.

Ejemplo: She shopped all day.

Did she shop all day?

1. They listened to the radio last night.

____

2. He called her at 4:16 AM.

____

3. She studied English last year.

____

4. I started at 8:00 this morning.

(you) _______________

5. They traveled a lot in March.

____

6. He visited his aunt last Saturday.

____

7. We camped in the desert.

(you) _______________

8. They looked for a new car last weekend.

____

Encontrará las respuestas en la página 49.

D. Escriba la letra de la pregunta delante de la respuesta correspondiente.

a. Did you pack yesterday?
b. Did you shop last Tuesday or Wednesday?
c. Who did you call last night?
d. What time did you start?
e. When did you arrive?
f. What did you do this morning?
g. Where did you camp?

Ejemplo: __a__ Yes, I packed all day yesterday.

______ 1. This morning I looked for a new car.

______ 2. We started at 7:00 AM.

______ 3. No, I shopped last Thursday.

______ 4. We camped at the beach in Florida.

______ 5. We arrived on Friday evening.

______ 6. I called my mother.

Diálogo 4

Encontrará las respuestas en la página 49.

Complete el diálogo.

Rosie You look tired.

Alex I ____________.

I studied all night. I have a test today.

Rosie ________ you have _________ English test?

Alex Yes, _________ 3:00 this afternoon.

What ____________ you do last night?

Rosie I ____________ TV and talked with my son _______ daughter.

Alex How old _________ your children?

Rosie My son ______ six and _____ daughter is nine.

Alex ___________ are their names?

Rosie Derek and Sonya. I have a picture.
We traveled to Colorado last summer.

Alex What did you ________ in Colorado?

Rosie We walked a lot.

Alex ________ you camp in the mountains?

Rosie No, we ___________ in a motel. It was fun.

4 Examen

Encontrará las respuestas en la página 49.

Lea el horario de Raúl y luego conteste a las preguntas.

Raúl's Schedule

Sun.	Mon.	Tue.	Wed.	Thurs.	Fri.	Sat.
	• pack • study English at 8:00 PM	• shop • call Annie	• play soccer	• visit Alex • call brother	• leave on vacation	

Ejemplo: Did Raúl pack on Tuesday?

No, he didn't. He packed on Monday.

1. What time did Raúl study English on Monday?

____

2. Did Raúl shop on Wednesday?

____

3. Who did he call on Tuesday?

____

Encontrará las respuestas en la página 49.

4. What did he do on Wednesday?

____

5. When did he call his brother?

____

6. Did he visit Alex on Monday?

____

7. Did he play soccer on Wednesday or Thursday?

____

8. Did he leave on vacation on Friday?

____

Vocabulario

A.
1. tried
2. played
3. looked for
4. packed
5. stopped
6. listened
7. arrived
8. traveled
9. called
10. wanted
11. showed
12. studied

B.
1. He didn't play basketball.
2. They didn't shop all day.
3. We didn't walk a lot.
4. I didn't pack yesterday.
5. She didn't talk to her sister on Tuesday.
6. They didn't listen to the radio.
7. It didn't rain last weekend.
8. You didn't look for it all morning.

Clase

C.
1. Did they listen to the radio last night?
2. Did he call her at 4:16 AM?
3. Did she study English last year?
4. Did you start at 8:00 this morning?
5. Did they travel a lot in March?
6. Did he visit his aunt last Saturday?
7. Did you camp in the desert?
8. Did they look for a new car last weekend?

D.
1. f
2. d
3. b
4. g
5. e
6. c

Diálogo

Rosie	You look tired.
Alex	I am. I studied all night. I have a test today.
Rosie	Do you have an English test?
Alex	Yes, at 3:00 this afternoon. What did you do last night?
Rosie	I watched TV and talked with my son and daughter.
Alex	How old are your children?
Rosie	My son is six and my daughter is nine.
Alex	What are their names?
Rosie	Derek and Sonya. I have a picture. We traveled to Colorado last summer.
Alex	What did you do in Colorado?
Rosie	We walked a lot.
Alex	Did you camp in the mountains?
Rosie	No, we stayed in a motel. It was fun.

Examen

1. He studied English at 8:00 PM.
2. No, he didn't. He shopped on Tuesday.
3. He called Annie.
4. He played soccer.
5. He called his brother on Thursday.
6. No, he didn't. He visited Alex on Thursday.
7. He played soccer on Wednesday.
8. Yes, he did.

Notas

V

Aprendamos viajando

V Notas

Encontrará las respuestas en la página 55.

New Orleans

Antes de completar este ejercicio, vea la sección "Aprendamos viajando" incluida en el video y lea la misma sección en el manual.

Si la información contenida en la oración es verdadera, haga un círculo alrededor de la palabra *True*. Si la información es falsa, haga un círculo alrededor de la palabra *False* y escriba una oración con la información correcta.

True *False* 1. New Orleans is a busy city every day.

____

True *False* 2. The German influence is everywhere in New Orleans.

____

True *False* 3. New Orleans is built on the Mississippi River.

____

True *False* 4. There are no boats on the river.

____

True *False* 5. You can take a carriage through Jackson Square.

____

Encontrará las respuestas en la página 55.

True *False* 6. The French Quarter is the heart of New Orleans.

____

True *False* 7. Preservation Hall is a good place to shop.

____

True *False* 8. Lafayette Cemetery is part of the business district.

____

True *False* 9. You can see the swamps by air boat.

____

True *False* 10. A bayou is a swamp.

____

True *False* 11. New Orleans is famous for its food.

____

True *False* 12. New Orleans is a fun city for tourists.

____

Respuestas V

1. True.
2. False. There is a lot of French influence.
3. True.
4. False. There are many boats on the river.
5. True.
6. True.
7. False. Preservation Hall is a music hall.
8. False. Lafayette Cemetery is in the Garden District.
9. True.
10. False. A bayou is a slow-moving stream.
11. True.
12. True.

C Notas

Aprendamos conversando

Notas

Aprendamos conversando C

Encontrará las respuestas en la página 64.

Actividad 1. Citas: los días, los meses y las estaciones del año

Diga qué día es la cita.

Sun.	Mon.	Tue.	Wed.	Thurs.	Fri.	Sat.
	• pack • study English at 8:00 PM	• shop • call Annie	• play soccer	• visit Alex • call brother	• leave on vacation	

I'll meet you on ___________.

See you in ___________.

Let's get together in the ___________.

Actividad 2. Hoy, ayer y mañana

Repita qué día es hoy y luego diga qué día fue ayer y qué día es mañana.

Today is ___________.

Yesterday was ___________.

Tomorrow is ___________.

Actividad 3. Este mes, el mes pasado y el mes que viene

Repita el nombre de este mes y luego diga el nombre del mes pasado y del mes que viene.

This month is ___________.

Last month was ___________.

Next month is ___________.

Actividad 4. ¿Qué tiempo hace hoy?

Escuche los sonidos o lo que dicen las personas y escoja la descripción correcta del pronóstico del tiempo.

1. It's raining.	It's snowing.
2. It's thundering.	It's windy.
3. It's sunny.	It's cloudy.
4. It's hot and humid.	There's a storm.
5. It's foggy.	It's sunny.
6. It's cold.	It's warm.

C Aprendamos conversando

Encontrará las respuestas en la página 64.

Actividad 5. Weather: formas alternativas
Escuche y repita.

The weather is nice.	The weather is bad.
It's a nice day.	The weather is terrible.
It's nice outside.	The weather is lousy.
It's a beautiful day.	It's a terrible day.
It's a gorgeous day.	It's ugly outside.

Actividad 6. Diálogos
Escuche los diálogos y haga una línea que conecte cada frase con el nombre correcto.

Diálogo 1

1. Today is his birthday.	Janet
2. Their birthday is September 5. (pick 2)	Bill
3. She's Bill's daughter.	Mark
4. He's meeting his wife and son for lunch.	Cindy
5. He's Amy's son.	

Diálogo 2

	Sonia
1. She was angry.	Peter
2. She was hungry.	Barbara
3. They were arguing. (pick 2)	Karen
4. She was talking on the phone.	Blake

Aprendamos conversando C

Encontrará las respuestas en la página 64.

Diálogo 3

1. This person called yesterday.
2. This person wasn't home.
3. This person played soccer.
4. This person is a good student.

Robert

Kathy

Diálogo 4

1. She needs a vacation.
2. She went to Florida with Bill.
3. She liked the beaches.
4. She played volleyball.

Amy

Ann

Actividad 7. La fecha

Escuche y escriba la fecha correcta. Use el número correspondiente al mes y el número correspondiente al día.

1. 3/1
2. ______
3. ______
4. ______
5. ______
6. ______
7. ______
8. ______
9. ______
10. ______

July

Sun	Mon	Tue	Wed	Thur	Fri	Sat
1	2	3	4	5	6	7
8	9	10	11	12	13	14
15	16	17	18	19	20	21
22	23	24	25	26	27	28
29	30	31				

Aprendamos conversando

Actividad 8. ¿Qué estaban haciendo?

Escuche y responda las preguntas sobre los horarios de Edward y Ellen. Busque la información en los horarios de abajo.

last week	Mon.	Tues.	Wed.	Thurs.	Fri.	Sat.	Sun.
Edward's Schedule	2 PM meet w/Bob	12 PM lunch w/Susan	8 PM dinner w/sister	8:30AM breakfast w/Sam	7 PM shop for Gary's present	3 PM play soccer	1 PM visit John & Linda
Ellen's Schedule	9 AM call my sisters	12 PM clean house	1 PM lunch w/Carol	2 PM visit Pedro	11 AM shop for food 7 PM shop for Gary's present	9 AM call my cousins	4 PM cook a chicken dinner

Actividad 9. ¿Qué hicieron?

Escuche y conteste más preguntas sobre el horario de Edward y Ellen. Refiera al mismo horario.

Sunday
4 PM

Saturday
3 PM

Monday
2 PM

Aprendamos conversando C

Encontrará las respuestas en la página 65.

Actividad 10. Rock Around the Clock: pronunciación
Escuche y marque con un círculo la palabra que oiga.

lock	luck	shot	shut
dock	duck	cot	cut
sock	suck	got	gut
hot	hut	cop	cup
not	nut		

Actividad 11. El pronóstico del tiempo
Escuche el reporte sobre las condiciones climatológicas de un día en cinco ciudades diferentes de los Estados Unidos y conteste las preguntas. Escriba el nombre de la(s) ciudad(es) correcta(s).

New York   Los Angeles   Chicago   San Antonio   Miami

1. Which cities have thunderstorms in the report?

   ________ ________ ________

2. What city has high of 82 degrees and a low of 70 degrees?

   ____

3. Where is it very hot today and tomorrow?

   ____

4. Where is it cloudy?

   ________ ________ ________

5. Which cities are sunny?

   ________ ________

6. What city has a low temperature of 63 degrees?

   ____

Actividad 4.

1. It's raining.	It's snowing.
2. It's thundering.	It's windy.
3. It's sunny.	It's cloudy.
4. It's hot and humid.	There's a storm.
5. It's foggy.	It's sunny.
6. It's cold.	It's warm.

Actividad 6.

Diálogo 1

1. Today is his birthday.
2. Their birthday is September 5. (pick 2)
3. She's Bill's daughter.
4. He's meeting his wife and son for lunch.
5. He's Amy's son.

Janet
Bill
Mark
Cindy

Diálogo 2

1. She was angry.
2. She was hungry.
3. They were arguing. (pick 2)
4. She was talking on the phone.

Sonia
Peter
Barbara
Karen
Blake

Diálogo 3

1. This person called yesterday.
2. This person wasn't home.
3. This person played soccer.
4. This person is a good student.

Robert
Kathy

Diálogo 4

1. She needs a vacation.
2. She went to Florida with Bill.
3. She liked the beaches.
4. She played volleyball.

Amy
Ann

Actividad 7.

1. 3/1
2. 9/22
3. 4/12
4. 2/27
5. 10/23
6. 7/4
7. 1/14
8. 5/10
9. 6/13
10. 12/25

Actividad 10.

lock	(luck)	shot	(shut)
(dock)	duck	cot	(cut)
(sock)	suck	(got)	gut
hot	(hut)	cop	(cup)
not	(nut)		

Actividad 11.

1. Which cities have thunderstorms in the report?

   New York   Chicago   Miami

2. What city has high of 82 degrees and a low of 70 degrees?

   New York

3. Where is it very hot today and tomorrow?

   San Antonio

4. Where is it cloudy?

   New York   Chicago   Miami

5. Which cities are sunny?

   Los Angeles   San Antonio

6. What city has a low temperature of 63 degrees?

   Chicago

Notas

Notas

Respuestas

1. (e) 2/14/2003
2. (b) December 16th
3. (a) May, June, July
4. (c) The day before yesterday was
5. (d) were shopping
6. (c) Were, sleeping
7. (b) No, he wasn't.
8. (a) snow
9. (d) Is it
10. (b) Yes, it was.
11. (e) 36°
12. (a) Last weekend
13. (c) looked for
14. (c) Did, study
15. (d) Yes, I did.

Examen final 4

Llene el círculo correspondiente a la respuesta correcta.

1. February 14, 2003 ________
- O a) 14/3/2002
- O b) 2/14/2004
- O c) 2003/14/2
- O d) 2003/2/14
- O e) 2/14/2003

2. His birthday is 12/16. ______
- O a) November eleventh
- O b) December 16th
- O c) December 11th
- O d) December twelfth
- O e) November 15th

3. April, __________________
- O a) May, June, July
- O b) September, October, December
- O c) January, March, August
- O d) May, July, August
- O e) March, May, June

4. Today is August 15th. ________ *August 13th.*
- O a) Yesterday was
- O b) Tomorrow is
- O c) The day before yesterday was
- O d) The day before yesterday
- O e) The day after tomorrow is

*5. They*__________ *all weekend.*
- O a) was shopping
- O b) wasn't
- O c) shopping
- O d) were shopping
- O e) isn't shopping

6. ___ *you* ___ *yesterday at 3:00?*
- O a) Did, calling
- O b) Do, sleeping
- O c) Were, sleeping
- O d) Are, sleep
- O e) Is, sleep

7. Was he sick yesterday? _______
- O a) No, he was.
- O b) No, he wasn't.
- O c) Sick.
- O d) Yes, sick.
- O e) Yes, yesterday.

8. There was __ *outside this morning.*
- O a) snow
- O b) rainy
- O c) clouds
- O d) sunny
- O e) storms

9. ________________ *cloudy?*
- O a) Are there
- O b) Is there
- O c) Are they
- O d) Is it
- O e) Was there

10. Was it sunny on Saturday?
- O a) No, there weren't.
- O b) Yes, it was.
- O c) Yes, it is.
- O d) Yes, it does.
- O e) No, it isn't.

11. The temperature is ________.
- O a) 36th
- O b) the 36º
- O c) thirty-sixth degree
- O d) about 36
- O e) 36º

12. _____ *it was windy and cold.*
- O a) Last weekend
- O b) Next weekend
- O c) Next Thursday
- O d) A little
- O e) Tomorrow

13. I _____ *my book all morning.*
- O a) stopped
- O b) listened to
- O c) looked for
- O d) arrived
- O e) traveled

14. ___ *he* ___ *English last year?*
- O a) Did, studying
- O b) Do, studying
- O c) Did, study
- O d) Do, learn
- O e) Does, studying

15. Did you go to school yesterday?
____
- O a) No, to school.
- O b) No, I did.
- O c) No, today.
- O d) Yes, I did.
- O e) To school.

ındo termine el examen, córtelo en la línea de puntos y envíelo a:

Profesores
640 S. San Vicente Boulevard
Los Angeles, California 90048-4618
U.S.A.

· favor, escriba claramente su nombre y dirección (use tinta oscura) a que podamos enviarle el examen corregido.

ombre ____________________

irección ____________________

iudad ______________ Estado ____________

ódigo Postal __________ País ____________

lo prefiere, puede enviarlo por fax al (323) 782-7466.
esponderemos por fax.
ı fax(______) ______________

Si desea saber las respuestas de una forma inmediata, visite nuestra página Web, www.isbonline.com, y haga el examen en el Internet.

Si tiene alguna pregunta, envíe un correo electrónico a:
profesores@isbonline.com
Este servicio no está disponible en el estado de California.

Fecha ____________________

Nº. de contrato ____________________

Teléfono (_______) ____________